MAKING SENSE OF BEHAVIOUR

NOT ME, MISS!

The Truth about Children who Lie

by

Rob Long

A NASEN PUBLICATION

Published in 2000

ISBN 1 901485 13 7

Published by NASEN.
NASEN is a company limited by guarantee, registered in England and Wales. Company No. 2674379.
NASEN is a registered charity. Charity No. 1007023.

Further copies of this book and details of NASEN's many other publications may be obtained from the Publications Department at its registered office: NASEN House, 4/5 Amber Business Village, Amber Close, Amington, Tamworth, Staffs. B77 4RP.
Tel: 01827 311500; Fax: 01827 313005
Email: welcome@nasen.org.uk; Website: www.nasen.org.uk

Cover design by Raphael Creative Design.
Typeset in Times by J. C. Typesetting and printed in the United Kingdom by Stowes (Stoke-on-Trent).

Contents

Preface

NOT ME, MISS! The Truth about Children who Lie is one of eight booklets in the series *Making Sense of Behaviour* by Rob Long. The others are *Exercising Self-control; Developing Self-esteem through Positive Entrapment for Pupils facing Emotional and Behavioural Difficulties; Friendships; Understanding and Supporting Depressed Children and Young People; Supporting Pupils with Emotional and Behavioural Difficulties through Consistency;* and *Learning to Wave: Some Everyday Guidelines for Stress Management.*

The first five titles give practical ideas and information for teachers to use with children with worrying behaviours in their classes. These are written to help teachers both understand and change some of the difficulties that children might experience (depression, lack of self-control, low self-esteem, friendship problems and lying).

Challenging Confrontation gives information and techniques for teachers to use when dealing with argumentative, angry and difficult pupils. *Supporting Pupils with Emotional and Behavioural Difficulties through Consistency* advocates a whole-school approach for low-level misbehaviours whilst *Learning to Wave* is written for teachers themselves. It contains advice about coping with the stress which might arise from dealing with children with behavioural problems.

Each book stands alone but when read as a set the behavioural issues and their solutions overlap and this emphasises the need for positive and consistent strategies to be put into place throughout the school.

Acknowledgements
The author and publishers wish to express their grateful thanks to Lorna Johnston, Agnes Donnelly and Dorothy Smith for their helpful suggestions and comments.

Not Me, Miss!
The Truth about Children who Lie

Introduction

Picture the scene. In the Head's office sits a young child in tears. The child tells how a class mate has bitten their arm, with no provocation whatsoever.

Next into the office is the accused who gives a very different account of how the other child had pushed, teased and hit them. The bite was an act of self-defence.

Under such circumstances it can be very difficult to disentangle the truth. There are times when school staff have to deal with children and young people whose inability to tell the truth becomes a growing concern.

From a distance we may think that 'a lie is a lie, is a lie.' But what children say and do can often carry a different message to the overt one. Behind many lies exists a child's basic hopes and fears. The lie often reflects how they would like things to be.

Why children lie is as complicated as any other aspect of human behaviour. There can be several reasons for any single piece of behaviour. (For example, there could be several reasons to explain why you are reading this booklet.) A common explanation for lying is that it is an attempt to avoid punishment for a wrongdoing, but there are many other reasons.

This booklet will provide a framework to enable 'the lie' to be made sense of and to provide focused support to those pupils and students who use lies to cope with a wide range of needs and circumstances.

Understanding the reasons and motives for children lying helps us to appreciate how ambiguous behaviour can be. Three children could tell the same lie, but there would be a different reason for each of them and they would each need to be supported in a different way.

For example:

Where is your homework?

Claire: I have done it but I lost it on the way to school.
I tried to do it but it was too hard, but I can't admit that to you.

Tom: I have done it but I lost it on the way to school.
My friends called on me and I didn't want to miss going out to have fun with them.

Dean: I have done it but I lost it on the way to school.
Mum and Dad had a terrible fight last night and the last thing I could think about was homework.

Learning to lie

The value of telling the truth is normally learned in the home. But children can be taught mixed messages about lying.

Firstly when they express their feelings honestly, 'I hate my sister', they can be told not to say such nasty things as they don't really mean it. Children can quickly learn that it is better to lie than to say what they really feel. A more helpful approach is for them to learn that there are times when 'if you can't say anything nice, then don't say anything at all.' (Sometimes 'no comment' is the best comment.)

Secondly children can learn that when they do tell the truth they will be punished. For example, when a child finally confesses to having broken the vase, they may be grounded for a week and sent immediately to their room. The lesson learnt can be that telling the truth resulted in punishment, whereas lying avoided punishment.

Why do children lie?

To make sense of why children lie we need to understand some key aspects of child development. These overlap and relate to each other as the figure below suggests.

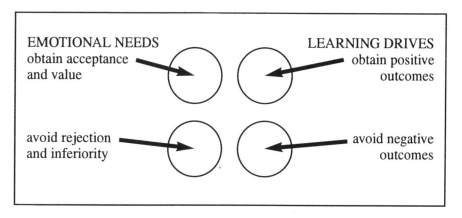

EMOTIONAL NEEDS
obtain acceptance
and value

LEARNING DRIVES
obtain positive
outcomes

avoid rejection
and inferiority

avoid negative
outcomes

There are then two relevant aspects controlling and influencing how children develop. These are their internal emotional needs and their ability to learn.

All children have fundamental emotional needs:

- to gain acceptance and feel valued

- to avoid rejection and feelings of inferiority

This need to belong and to feel valued can be seen as the motivation for certain types of lying.

Namely lying to:

- enhance status
- be in control
- displace anger
- hurt others

Learning is the second key process that strongly influences us. We learn that certain behaviours lead to positive outcomes and others to unpleasant ones. Children are motivated towards those behaviours that obtain pleasure and to avoid those that cause pain. Children learn through their experiences at home and with other significant adults, including media figures, the value of telling the truth. Such learning can be seen in other types of lying.

Namely lying to:

- avoid doing something I don't like
- avoid being punished
- avoid the reactions of adults

All children make up stories and sometimes they can have difficulties distinguishing fact from fantasy. This ability will be part of their normal learning. It would be wrong to classify such as lying. By lying we usually mean a conscious act of deception. (Though as we will see there can be times when a child may lie and not be conscious of doing so because it is a learned habit.)

The value of telling the truth
It is important to remember that the fact that children lie often shows that they are aware that they have done something wrong. The child that does not either understand, care or fear the consequences does not lie. Children who lie know what is wrong but are unable to resist temptation. When we know that a child is vulnerable to lying we need to catch them telling the truth and praise them. Tell them how proud we are that they 'owned up when lying might have been an easier option'. (See Appendix 1.)

The role of punishment
Punishment is a difficult issue. If children know that the adults who care for them are volatile and likely to shout excessively, then it is not surprising that some children will lie to avoid such outbursts. Children need to know that their accounts are listened to and their efforts to be honest and truthful will be valued. If children are always punished for lying then we may be teaching them not to get caught. The way forward is not to over-focus on the lie itself, but the reason for the lie.

Strictly speaking lying is 'punishment-avoidance behaviour'. The child's solution to the fear of punishment is to lie. Therefore when we punish children for lying we can unwittingly become part of the reason for them lying.

To the child, punishment becomes associated with being found out and not lying. Next time the child may find new and elaborate ways of avoiding telling the truth. (Remember the politicians who have been 'economical with the truth'.)

Compulsive lying

Compulsive lying can be an early indicator of more severe problems. These include social behaviour disorders, conduct disorder and attention deficit disorder. Usually a child will have a range of other behavioural disorders, such as:

- stealing
- cheating
- truanting
- aggression
- poor anger control
- impulsivity
- inability to link consequences with behaviour
- inattentiveness

Lying can also be used to cover up other serious problems such as drug or alcohol abuse. Adolescents with such difficulties will lie repeatedly to hide the truth about where they were, who they were with and what they have spent their money on. When a number of these difficulties co-exist together it is advisable to seek further advice and support, either from your school psychological service, GP or child guidance centre.

Lying, defence mechanisms and adolescents

We all rely at times on defence mechanisms to see things as we would like them to be, rather than how they really are. It takes confidence and a measure of critical awareness, to own up to having done something wrong. To protect our self-esteem we use mechanisms, such as:

Denial: 'What problem?'
Rationalisation: 'If I'd only had more time.'
Projection: 'It was your fault.'

There will be times therefore when children, especially those with a low self-esteem, will be self-motivated to lie as a way of protecting their weak self-images. This will also enable them to avoid taking responsibility for their behaviour. They will not necessarily be aware of this and their distortion of reality needs sensitive handling. This is especially true during adolescence.

Lying during adolescence can serve such functions as:

- avoidance of responsibility
- increase of excitement

Lying for many adolescents is seen as 'risky behaviour'. Lying and being generally deceptive fits in well with the young person's image. Our challenge is to help the student see pro-social behaviours, being honest, as being equally risky and therefore attractive.

- Being honest is risky
- Being honest takes strength

The double bind strategy
Sommers-Flanagan and Sommers-Flanagan (1997) use an example of how an understanding of the needs and fears of adolescents can be used to confront their needs and honesty.

> 'I guess for you it is safer to lie about stealing. I don't blame you for being afraid to admit that you went ahead and stole something. You had promised your parents and Social Worker that you wouldn't steal again.'

Adolescents do not like having to admit being scared or anxious. So when faced with the above they will either:

> Admit that lying is a safe option.
> Or
> Deny that lying is a safe option.

If the adolescent admits that lying was the safe option they can be encouraged to take 'risks' in being honest. They can be challenged or dared to become 'pro-social risk takers'.

(Those that deny that lying is a safe option can be encouraged to confess to reduce the punishments they will earn.)

Types of lying

As there are different motives for lying we must remember that why children lie can indicate how we will be able to best help them.

The examples below highlight this point.

Example 1
Lying to increase status
Sarah has been telling her friends about the horse that her father has just bought for her. She feeds and rides it each morning and is hoping to enter jumping competitions.

Sarah lives in a flat with her mother and sees her father every four weeks. There is no horse. Sarah is probably trying to increase her sense of value and importance with her friends.

Example 2
Lying for confrontation
In technology John rarely brings the correct equipment. When challenged by his teacher John explains that it has all been stolen. The teacher doubts this and John becomes increasingly angry when he realises that he is not being believed by his teacher.

Example 3
Habitual lying
Tom seems to lie whenever questioned by an adult. There can often seem to be no sense in his lying. He lies about his school work, his home life, his hobbies. When challenged with firm evidence he just laughs it off, and says that he was only 'joking anyway'.

As you work your way through the six different types of lying presented below your aim is to find the 'best fit' for the child you have in mind. It is worth noting that if we try to see the world through children's eyes their behaviour makes sense. Most children are trying to solve the challenges they meet. Regretfully they often find mistaken solutions. Lying is just such an example.

Use the Record Form in the appendix as an aide-memoir.

1. Habitual
Some children can very quickly learn a habit that at first meets a need, but when this disappears, the habit remains. In such children lying is almost a reflex reaction. This type of lying does respond to punishment. This is because punishment is designed to prevent a learned response. But on its own it will not work as it does not teach the child alternative ways to behave. It needs to be combined with care, compassion and new ways of responding.

Indicative questions
Does the child:

- lie when it is not in their interest to do so?
- lie in a wide range of dissimilar situations?
- promise to improve but with little success?
- overreact when challenged?
- show little response to rewards or punishments?

Strategies
i) Use stories involving similar behaviours to those the child does. Discuss outcomes with the child and look for alternatives.
ii) Develop a contract for the child not to lie. The contract should include a range of acceptable behaviours as well as positive and negative consequences.
iii) Establish three alternatives for the child to use when challenged with a cost to each one. For example:
> Time to think - Earns agreed activity
> Truthful response - Verbal praise
> Denial - Break time discussion
iv) Always show signs of having difficulty in accepting what the child is saying. 'Just have a think about what you're telling me, I'll be back in a few minutes.' Allow the child to retract with no fear of punishment.
v) Each day ask the child for small accounts of what they have done, where they have been etc? Give them practice at responding honestly to everyday questions and to learn a new habit.

2. Confrontational

For some children lying reflects a growing awareness on their part that adults cannot 'see inside them'. Becoming aware of this can result in some children enjoying the excitement that lying can produce. Such children can appear to act out an internal script, of being 'victim'. They will use attack as the best form of defence, accusing the adult of 'picking on them', or never 'believing what they say'.

Indicative questions
Does the child:

- readily argue with adults?
- lie to adults rather than peers?
- rarely back down?

- talk calmly about the issue?
- lie more with specific adults?

Strategies
i) Explain quietly that you are having some trouble understanding all of their account and could they write it out in full for you with more detail?
ii) a) Only challenge them when you have conclusive evidence, 'I saw you break the pencil.'
   b) Only challenge with a colleague present.
iii) Make time to develop a relationship with the child. Find common interests and spend time together.
iv) Show surprise that they should lie to you. Discuss with them a range of options that you will use when there is a situation where they have lied. Give them some options to enable them to 'save face'.

3. Avoiding consequences and responsibility

Some children lie to avoid the consequences that they 'believe' will happen to them. Perhaps they have been severely punished in the past. They can also have difficulties in understanding the consequences of their behaviour.

Indicative questions
Does the child:

- rarely lie to avoid punishments?
- accept the consequences of actions?
- accept punishment?
- accept responsibility?
- know how their behaviour affects others?

Strategies
i) Make an 'honesty contract' with the child and set out a range of rewards for not lying.
ii) Help the child keep a self-monitoring diary to increase awareness of all the times when they told the truth, despite being tempted to lie.
iii) With the child develop a number of 'paybacks' for when they do lie. (Take care that these are not rewarding.) Paint a picture during breaktime, do some cleaning; so that they know exactly what will happen to them if they do lie.
iv) Teach them ways to slow down their actions so that they STOP, THINK and then DECIDE what to do.

v) Use role play to set up situations where a child may be tempted to lie.
    Broken a favourite family object.
    Lost a toy borrowed from a friend.
    Forgotten to pass on an important message.
    Failed to keep a date with a friend.
Discuss with the child the different ways of responding in such situations; how would different choices affect different people?

4. Status

Self-esteem in children is very vulnerable. Each day they can take 'knocks and bumps' that chip away at how they feel. When faced with a difficult situation where the outcome could be expected to embarrass or humiliate them, it is hardly surprising that some choose to lie to protect their self-worth. It can become a vicious circle though, resulting in a loss of self-esteem.

Indicative questions
Does the child:

- work well independently?
- show confidence in new situations?
- belong to a friendship group?
- have good social skills?
- know their positive skills?

Strategies
i) Check that the student does not have learning difficulties and is lying to avoid failing.
ii) Give the student extra time to review successes and set new achievable targets.
iii) Promote the child's self-worth through giving positions of responsibility and valuing their efforts as well as their achievements.
iv) Do 'Life Mapping' with them to show them the many achievements and successes that they have already experienced.
v) Teach the child a range of positive self-statements. For example:
    One thing I am good at ...
    A success I recently had was ...
    My friends like me because ...
Also teach relaxation techniques to develop self-control in emotionally difficult situations.

5. Attention seeking

All children seek attention, especially infants. Some children develop a need for excessive attention, and lying can sometimes be used to achieve this. These children want people to notice them and want to be treated as being special. Often such children can annoy adults, who become trapped into giving them a disproportionate amount of attention for inappropriate behaviour. Ignore the unwanted behaviour but give lots of attention when the child behaves correctly. Attention seeking is a description of the problem behaviour - not the child.

Indicative questions
Does the child:

• become upset when punished?
• willingly follow instructions?
• make you feel relaxed and unstressed?
• make you feel confident that your efforts will succeed?
• rarely receive attention?

Strategies
i) If the child tells fantastic stories with little relationship to reality ask them to either write them down or draw a picture.
ii) Pair the child with a peer who works to obtain attention appropriately. Make sure that you give the pupil your attention strictly on your terms.
iii) Avoid engaging in long discussions over stories told by the pupil.
iv) Keep a log of the time lost through lies and stories told by the pupil. Agree with the pupil that lost learning time will have to be 'paid back' later by them missing some free time.
v) Keep a range of varied rewards that the pupil is given whenever you believe they responded well. Initially give rewards frequently but then make them more random. This will avoid dependency and help the child learn the value of being honest.

6. Revenge

The child who tells lies about peers with the intention of getting them into trouble is probably motivated by revenge. Such children are often lonely and socially isolated from their peers. They may believe that they have been hurt and now want others to feel the same pain they have experienced. A goal will be to raise the child's self-esteem. (See also the strategies presented earlier under Status.)

Indicative questions
Does the child:

- relate well with peers?
- help others?
- enjoy the challenge of new situations?
- empathise with others?
- make you feel relaxed and at ease?

Strategies
i) Construct ways of increasing the child's sense of belonging to a group.
ii) Arrange a buddy system to help the child improve peer relationships. Help the child to see the different behaviours that the role model does and the consequences to them. 'Do you notice what happened to Sam when he lent Jane his ruler?'
iii) Discuss concerns with the child, situations that are difficult, and produce a range of alternatives.
iv) Encourage the child to share any interests or special skills with peers.
v) Use story techniques. Tell a story where there is a child who lies about friends. How is the child who is lying feeling? How will the children who are being lied about feel? Aim to increase the child's understanding of the emotional consequences of their behaviour to both them and others.

Promoting honesty: some ideas

Below are some ideas/activities to be used to help show children the value of being honest and some of the skills they will need.

The truth game
In this game everyone is free to say whatever they like, whether it is true or not. Teacher might say 'It's time to go home,' when it isn't. Or they might say 'Let's watch a video now.' But then say they didn't mean it. (After such a game the value of telling the truth is well established.)

Ann's story
Ann thought making up stories was a good way to make friends and keep them interested in her. Nobody who knew her, knew when she was being honest or not. One day Ann saw a house being broken into and ran for help. But nobody came to help because they all thought it was 'just another one of Ann's stories'.

16

The benefits of honesty - some ideas for discussion
- I feel good
- Shows strength
- People can trust me
- I am taking responsibility for what I do
- Any punishment will be fair
- I will learn better ways of coping with difficulties

The burden of lying - some ideas for discussion
- I will not like myself
- Shows weakness
- People will not trust me
- I will be punished for lying as well
- It's the soft option
- I will have to rely on lying

Problem solving
Lying is used by many children as their only solution to a problem. 'I knew Dad would say "No", so I lied.' In reality Dad would have wanted more information. Teach children a range of age-appropriate problem-solving skills.

```
STOP ──► THINK ──► CHOOSE ──► EVALUATE
        GOOD CHOICE   or   BAD CHOICE
```

We need more and more today to understand the competing messages that children and young people receive. Honesty can have many shades just as lying can have many different purposes. Unless we understand the nature and function of lying we may either overreact or underreact when faced with children who lie. We may need to support children who have learned a different standard at home - as the old saying puts it, 'What parents do moderately, children do to excess.' This booklet has explored the reasons behind, 'Not me, Miss!' and how to support children who don't always find 'honesty the best policy'.

PROMOTING HONESTY

STUDENT'S NAME..

COMPLETED BY..

INFORMATION
Where does the lying occur? ....

Who is it usually to?　　| adults |　　| family |　　| peers |

Is there a theme or topic to the lying?

| clothes |　| money |　| friends |　| school work |　| other |

Are there excessive pressures on the child at home or school?...........

Does the child understand 'lying'?......................................

DOES THE ABOVE INFORMATION SUGGEST ANY IMMEDIATE CHANGES?

PROBLEM SOLVING
Is the child's lying motivated by:

Attention ....'I would like more of your time.'
Status..........................'I need to feel important.'
Revenge......................'I want others to feel as hurt as I do.'
Confrontation ....'I would like to fight.'
Habit...........................'I always lie.'
Fear ....'I am frightened of being punished.'

STRATEGIES CHOSEN

REVIEW BY DATE..

References

Brooks, J. (1994) *Parenting in the 90's*, Mayfield Publishing Company: Mountain View, California, USA.

Mellor, N. (1997) *Attention Seeking*, Lucky Duck Publishing: Bristol.

Sommers-Flanagan, J. & Sommers-Flanagan, R. (1997) *Tough Kids, Cool Counselling*, American Counselling Association: Virginia, USA.

Thompson, C. & Rudolph, L. (1992) *Counselling Children*, Brooks/Cole: Pacific Grove, California, USA.